landia

CELINA SU

in solidarity
& with love
Celina

ISBN: 978-0-9988439-1-9
Book design by Kiran Puri
Cover design by HR Hegnauer

Belladonna* is a reading and publication series that promotes the work of women writers who are adventurous, experimental, politically involved, multiform, multicultural, multi-gendered, impossible to define, delicious to talk about, unpredictable, & dangerous with language.

This book has been made possible in part by the Community of Literary Magazines and Presses' FACE OUT program with support from the Jerome Foundation as well as by the New York State Council on the Arts, the Leslie Scalapino - O Books Fund, the National Endowment for the Arts, and donations from individuals. Belladonna* is a proud member of CLMP.

Distributed to the trade by
Small Press Distribution
1341 Seventh Street
Berkeley, CA 94710
www.SPDBooks.org

Also available directly through
Belladonna* Collaborative
925 Bergen Street, Suite 405
Brooklyn, NY 11238
www.BelladonnaSeries.org

Library of Congress Cataloging-in-Publication Data

Names: Su, Celina, 1977- author.
Title: Landia / Celina Su.
Description: Brooklyn, N.Y. : Belladonna Collaborative, 2018.
Identifiers: LCCN 2017056055 | ISBN 9780998843919 (pbk. : alk. paper)
Classification: LCC PS3619.U285 A6 2018 | DDC 811/.6--dc23
LC record available at https://lccn.loc.gov/2017056055

*deadly nightshade, a cardiac and respiratory stimulant, having purplish-red flowers and black berries

for my mom
Christina Wen-Fong Tseng Su, 曾文風

&

for Justin Frederick Blinder, Perseu

TOPOGRAPHIES

DISTANCES

*A Book of
Questions*

TERRITORIES

TOPOGRAPHIES

To Steal Oneself

In between, an ellipsis of the agentic. Whereas

A smuggled adult is merely a smuggled adult.
Unless I, a woman of disgrace, open my mouth
Wide, illustrate the scars to prove it.
Then I exotic them my own. Dryly, would I.
Whose subjects, which objects,
Lit on fire as if *pristine* were a burning choice—

Finger-pointing these choices institutionalized.
Still my own luminous blackened cloud of...

A smuggled child, who is a trafficked child.
In certain circumstances of layaway purchase and sale,
Ringing up the will of others, limb-like devices
Perfect for crate-filled kitchen-friendly
Heavy lids on the school shift—

Double-Dutch me *victim* or *criminal*, skip the tumble,
Whose subject who objects to whose agent,
Prowling like a snuggled animal.
Metonymy fierce. Regal legal.
A snakehead with no mongoose federal agent,
A coyote's jowls with my own Benz bling
To ransack these entrapping escapes
Targeting darting person-shaped objects—

Tending to my wounds
Licking them quantitative
Number me dispassionate

Chai-Dan Submits Three Aims

For Chai-Dan and his family, Maehongson Province, Thailand

As if hailing from a documented birth. A nascent shiftless country. Not
       so evidently nicknamed—
border in an adopted language. To win asylum, to name three aims.

One. To take refuge in the imperfect. No, less perfect. Sitting in a
       hut, an appellation of near truth—
Counting the square meters. The mattress, the buckets, the
       lightbulb on a string.

Two. To slash leaves against the dirt ground. Living days on stilts—
To ground them into a roof of harshness. It protects us thus.

How does one reclaim an insult that has not yet been called—
Borderlines move daily. My legs lightning and yet. No path to
       a camp.

Two and a half, to construct houses without a name. Without
       numbers or years or—
To stand on the right side of the border, to hurry east. Still, fingers
as if
One possessed fading papers. Folded like a road map—
Pressed in plastic bags lined like onion skin. What documents
       me human.

Except my body outstretched, rock-gathering. To break into
       shards to mold into wetness—
To grow the river into concrete. To displace this place. To reap
       the rewards of infinite

fractions. 2.66 with a bar over it. To smooth this stuttering invisibility.

If   I am not legal nor here. Less a state—

I christen these escapes. To flee an integrating war. Into more a
     state of abject sustenance.

To unrealized factions, to flee this absence of bullet point goals.
     A determinate wage. Then my running evades name-calling—
(To belong nowhere is to steep oneself in ambiguity. To call
     myself. Realistic. Which liberation lies in illiteracy.) Still,

if only,

if   I do not list an occupation here. My laminated identity—

Replaces no names, to eke out to bequeath room to Number
     Three,

Route 1095

Maehongson Province, 2008

1. เข้าใจ
kao-jai
enter-heart

To understand. From Bangkok, it always takes me another two days to get here. Sitting in a bungalow in a rice field, listening. To fragile geckos trilling clicks, water buffaloes moaning, a creek slowly trickling, frogs croaking. The distant beats of trance music, the national anthem, the prayers of a mosque, the gongs and chants of a Buddhist temple, the silence of scarecrows. Always, two fans whirring.

I've been coming to northwestern Thailand to work with a small NGO working with Shan Burmese refugee children for close to ten years, and still. To enter one's heart is not necessarily to—

That ใจ (*jai*) signifies the "mind" as well as the "heart." That which it is closest to is what it is not.

2. ปลูกใจ
plook-jai
wake-heart

To rouse, to hearten to action. R- and K-, both Thai, were running an informal, illicit school for refugee children in the area. Without pay, for two years. Attendance hovered near 100% every day.

Later, the District Office shut down the informal school. R- and K- surreptitiously got the kids into Thai schools. Now, they are social workers rather than teachers. Cleaning blood off benches, dealing in maxi pads, collecting first bras in the Wednesday market, distributing shoes and uniforms, procuring birth certificates from the District Office. The Officer retorts, "Did you know it is illegal to help someone who is not in your family?"

3. ซื้อใจ
seeuu-jai
buy-heart

To influence via money. (My power here unsettling. A university degree, a couple of successful grant proposals, but mostly my passport. Discordant with how I look to the locals, so that they constantly point at my face and ask me where I'm from. Maybe I should work instead at "home," or in Latin America, where I first grew up, even if they thought that I looked like I was *actually* from... Where I can speak their language, perhaps navigate at least some social situations.)

R- and K- are getting restless, ready to move on, but still they work, partly because of the grants we raise. I am a heartless heart-buyer. They say that we make it "a real NGO"; they're the "normal workers helping the children."

4. เกรงใจ
greng-jai
dread-heart

To be fearful in approach. I fear that my heart isn't petrified enough. Yet. To heed endless songs of praise for *greng-jai* on pop radio, in shampoo commercials, in guidebooks, in my language textbooks. To hold everyday experiences in an ineffable politics of fear and wonder.

A friend of mine visited Isaan, northeastern Thailand. It wasn't until he left Isaan and arrived in Bangkok that he realized that he'd left his passport behind. The guesthouse owner took the 11 p.m. bus to arrive in Bangkok at 4 a.m. with his passport, then took the 5 a.m. bus to return to work.

Such awesome, dreadful hearts. From a murmured distance. When my friend visited Isaan again, months later, he learned that this guesthouse owner was abusive to her employees, especially the Cambodian refugee, and never paid her any wages. The employees plotted for months to help the refugee escape. Back to Cambodia. As they did so, they developed an ornate story about how she needed to leave in the middle of the night not to escape, but because of a convoluted "emergency," lest the guesthouse owner lose face in town. To grasp a poetry of prosaic subjection.

5. ใจเย็น
jai-yen
cool-heart

To be equanimous. To answer, when we ask whether they had any problems with Burmese soldiers, *No*. When we ask again. *Nah*. So long as, they paid half of their meager earnings to the *junta* as levied taxes. Provided that, they portered weapons for them every year. On the condition that rapes in neighboring villages haunted them only in their sleep.

To keep calm, to stay cool, to live without freezing. To have a say, to access, to share in one's crops. To slash-and-burn one's paradoxical haven. To suffer a tempered heart.

6. เย็นใจ
ken-jai
push-heart

To be stranded in an improvised life without resources. To stand up straight, to not have spots on your teeth, to keep all of your fingers, to live to be old, or just older. To learn to read, to think out loud, to storm one's brain. To be pulled as well as pushed.

To build a new hyper-flammable thatch hut each year and stay there, imbued by the sweet scent of defoliants, surrounded by fiery ants.

To walk farther each week, hunting rocks in the riverbed, carrying them to shore on your back, filling an entire truckbed every day. To pound them into powder, churn them into concrete, pour them into the foundation of a house for other people's children. To weigh your worth in stones.

7. ใจร้อน
jai-rawn
hot-heart

To be hot-tempered. Like me, graceless here, unable to read subtle social signals, unable to maneuver even slow-moving buses. Passing by, a baby, her father, her grandmother, and a dog atop a motorbike, whirling around the corner, a cartful of chickens clucking behind.

Two weeks after his hut burned down, we asked whether anything bad happened that year, and he could not think of anything. After his wife "found a new husband," after she walked for 5 days through the jungle only to land in jail for working without a permit, only a foreigner would bristle at such inconsequentials with a boiling heart. Let it dwell, and the heart will fracture a fever pitch (มีไข้ใจ, mi-kai-jai, "have-fever-heart"). To shatter with feeling.

8. กินแหนง
แคลงใจ

gin-naeng-
kleng-jai

use/eat,
suspect
doubt-heart

To be mutually suspicious. To cherish what is clearly a middle-income country. Malaria eradicated, HIV/ AIDS under control. The hushed, gleaming metro whooshes past. The ice in outdoor market guava shakes is o, so fine.

To struggle in a political economy where hairstyle magazines feature primers on currency devaluation, and 7-11 clerks banter about NGOs. Where lesbian women call themselves ทอมดี้ (tom-dee, "tomboy-lady") because "lesbian" now signifies "girl-on-girl action" for sex-pats. Where street food stalls announce "IMF" as a codeword for "austerity," for "bargain": ไก่ทอดIMF! (gai-tawt-IMF, "IMF fried chicken!") Through microcredit, the power of the market, the promise of a franchise.

The anatomical heart. To flinch at the structural violence, the "noncompliance" of mothers in getting their babies vaccinated. The refugees' most common afflictions, broken backs, pterygium (sun-scarred eyes), stunting from malnutrition, severed fingers and phantom pain. To leave the medical technology to the *farang*; it was theirs in the first place.

To maintain a right-sized heart. To be น้อย (noy, "small") is to nurse grudges, to be ยักษ์ (yak, "giant") is to turn brutal. But to be ใหญ่ (yai, "big") is merely tawdry, ostentatious.

To stand on the right side of the tempestuous border. In Laos, with plenty of leftover American bombshells to use as plant pots, lining restaurants, carpeting gardens. In Cambodia, where the blue beret United Nations soldiers, we are told, transitioned the country to democracy in the 1990s. They stand still now, holding onto sex workers in wax.

10. ใจดี
jai-di
good-heart

To be kind.

ดีใจ
di-jai
heart-good/
well

To be happy. An inversion of goodness, happiness. Teen pregnancy, drug abuse, gambling. To be pathologically social, playing with fate for a welling heart.

เห็นใจ
hen-jai
see-heart

To commiserate. To rewrite in translation. Not via seemingly seamless integration or romanticized pleasantries. To simultaneously disappear and paper my state of being—decoupage in the context of undocumented statelessness: As if haven were either literal or metaphorical, solace just begging for doctrine. To question legibility, whether what I wrote was what they read: My shirts have no colors. The tops of my ashen knees covered by dirt, as if this place could seep into my skin—Each coup or president or teacher calling our names, bringing me to the front of the class, rendering me an exhibit of—Those emblems that cannot be torn apart, co-opted, fucked and passed on, even with the beauty of half-blood.

To be surprised. My heart has normalized; it has cooled.

Really? จริงๆไหม? *Jing jing mai?* For Kamloo, Pao, Sangkor, Pai, Swaymud, Amporn, Taworn, who wrote. จริงใจ (jing-jai, "real heart"). To be sincere. To answer a thousand questions, we created new ones: About juntas on blurred-together days and rebel armies on blurry-eyed nights, about the theft of fears. About kicking *sepak* balls high into the air, wandering at night to peer at her secret burials of "lost" memories, the age called "eleven."

(The tickets were so expensive, 3,000 baht a person. So we walked for five days and five nights. In the jungle, two camouflaged giants gave us three balls of rice. My sister waiting patiently for her 8th birthday, for her turn to go to Bangkok, to join my aunt, to work—)

Each parenthetical a haunting sour stuck inside my mouth, tucked under my tongue, almost masked by the saccharine taste of pesticides from the garlic fields.

(My father was picking bamboo and feeding the buffaloes, but after two years we crossed into Thailand again when soldiers shot people near my—My mother is still ill, so she cannot touch rain water. And when these work permits run out, will we leave, will we go back to the border, will we live in a space between, drift alongside, vanish into a line we must cross again, and again, and.)

พแล้ะแม่ ขอ งผ ม แตก(จ)แยกกัน ไป

คนละ ที่ ละ ทาง ผม อยากน้ำ มีงา ?

รับผิดชอบคือ ล้างจาน   ผมชอบเ?

วิชา คณิตสาสตร์ และ ลิช ภาษาไทย

โตขึ้น ผม อยาก เป็น ทหาร   เพราะ

จะ ได้ ช่วยปองกัน ประเทศชาติ ของ

ตนเอง

A Model Citizen, Age 5

(When I grow up, I will become a Thai soldier, and I will arrest the Burmese migrant drug dealers, but their mothers will be very, very. With their sons in prison, because they cannot see them, for they are not evil.)

(I dream of growing watermelons.)

The Incessant of Travel

Day 1   I unravel in Phnom Penh.

Open arms, open plains. These terrains
where the nations united
do not pretend to keep peace.
The brutal face lies
not in the panopticon,
but in my own ability to
turn the other cheek. Then,
to the other side. I do it
one more time,
faster. I manage to *just say no*,
just like Nancy would have wanted me to.

A panoply of torture devices illuminated by incandescent signs,
prayed upon by touring evangelicals evoking God's will in the
    guest book,
a high percentage of missing limbs, succulent mines—

Night 2   I ride to them in darkness,

without any street or bicycle lights
amidst the trees. I hear
the neighbors' steel wheel spokes
only when they whoosh past me.
I arrive before dawn. A voice tells me
someone will steal my bicycle,
unless he watches it for me.
I tell this one-metered silhouette my name,
promise a small reward in return.

A dozen hours later,
two dozen street kids rush towards me.
"Celina, I watched your bicycle!"
"No, it was me, Celina. *I* watched your bicycle!"
What I did not buy:
shoes for the five-year-old postcard peddlers,
iced glass bottles of *saudade*. Fleetingly, they gave me
astringent sweets for a state of grace, only, missing the—

Week 3   I am still here, which means that my mind has wandered elsewhere.

The kids plead with me to cut out this hole.
Hard water, kidney stones, and infant melamine,
sight unseen. It is like the last wound
but in reverse,
its transient contours all the more searing.
To fathom the magnitude,
to count each as each before me,
pulling at my skirt,
holding my hands,
the pan-epic.
The difference between a module and a nodule
an interstitial slash, malignance made bureaucratic.

If I can't get to it,
let's at least shade it in.
Fetishize the artifice,
as if   it were.
A paracetamol to numb the phantom pain.
I come here because
I like the food, especially the tea leaf salad.
I will talk to my friends who live here, work here.
Our pleas without the pretty—

Seeing Like a State

I arrive two weeks early and buy a folding bicycle, light and
silver, for $50. (A few months later, I sell it back home in New
York, for a bit more than I paid for it.) I learn to ride it across the
street not according to the traffic lights, but according to when
other bicyclists do so; I ride it through the alleyways. I begin
to buy two wrong peaches from a man with a wheelbarrow. A
passer-by chides the vendor for handing me fruit that was about
to rot. I thank them, the vendor and the passer-by.

I ask a cab driver to take me to a specific neighborhood, reading
the pinyin in my *Lonely Planet* copy without the proper tones.
The driver stares at me, incredulous at what I do not know.

By the time my family arrives, one of the alley courtyards I'd
visited has been demolished. It wasn't one of the famous ones,
like Skewed Tobacco Pouch Street, South Gong and Drum Lane.
It didn't have any trinket shops, just homes, people. It may have
been there for 800 years. One small house remains, each of the
two rooms severed in half.

As if it were a dollhouse blown up to life
size, barely standing next to a middle-aged man in a white tee
shirt and rolled up pants. In the middle of the street in direct
sunlight, his face covered by the palms of his hands. I walk by
as quietly as I can, to give him privacy in what yesterday was
his living room. Where yesterday, at this hour, in this exact
spot, one felt a cool shade.

The day of my family's arrival, I travel to the airport with the aunt I have just met for the first time. I sit next to her in the car. She chants in low tones, *I'm going to see her. I'm going to see her.* At the airport, my grandmother and the ones who had remained behind—are left behind—stood next to one another, in the same building, same country, for the first time in sixty years. I expect a tearful homecoming, but instead, the conversation remains polite, focused on logistics, on getting through immigration, on who should go into which car to the restaurant. At the restaurant, I feel unnerved by the aquariums embedded in the marble floors, clumsy in my attempts to sidestep the koi swimming beneath my feet, even though a thick sheet of glass sits between us—The koi dramatically swerving from side to side in lines like high-pitched soundwaves.

—My relatives from the US and I walking across the vast, concrete plaza of heavenly peace. The outdoor thermostat announces that it is 44 degrees Celsius, 111 degrees Fahrenheit. Under yet another portrait of Mao, the family guide points at black dots on a new stick, upright on the horizon.

We are told that they are new ants on the hill, hailing from the Mongolian Wild West, trailing into different construction sites. Tiny speck workers, clearly not on spec. I wonder whether they would rather partake in a trade deficit. Without papers, nor what to write on them:

They told me it was an organized enterprise.
I came to the Beijing coast, fall off a cliff of a building—

I walked east to marry a new woman, leave my old one behind.
    I knew I would never see her again, and she—

        I squat on shared toilets, crisscrossed planks over pits of shit.
        I transform them into big ring roads.

I came here to look at the pale giants who live in the cities—
    They all rise half a meter taller than me—

I write my red story on a piece of white cardboard and sit on the sidewalk,
            watch them crowd around me—

They stand around, whisper bitter nothings amongst themselves.
The northern rolling Rs at the ends of their words a reminder,

This is not my home. Whether for emptiness, or in bile. So ill-distributed, these plights of fancy—Then make no mistake, these mistakes we can only—

Well, then. There are no aerial views, only fragmenting bodies. I see them inside, pink and iridescent heliotrope, flecked by black, curdled.

If the forbidden cityscape is corporeal, then it is a proper burial, the entrails of the buildings devouring themselves with a vengeance.

As if we were all tapeworms living off concrete and steel, tiny parasites so easily erased with digestion, defecation. *Rigor mortis*, softness in the want of.

(We are in the basin of Chimborazo and Carihuairazo and
Tungurahua and Cotopaxi, teetering on the edge of the Devil's
Nose. They thought that the neck of the moon was apocryphal,
or so I heard in the language of whispers.)

She tells me that she arrived from Fujian three weeks ago, that
she speaks no Spanish or English. Here, Casa China and Chifa
Pekin are numbers 17 and 27 of thirty-one restaurants ranked
in *Lonely Planet*, respectively. The older-generation workers
pretending to be second-generation pretending to be fifth-
generation explain that *ni chi fan* became *chifa, chau fan* became
chaufa. Add a wonton skin in the shape of a paper airplane on
top, call it "airport," the most popular dish in town. To devour
these spaces, ever in transit, this plaguing want for want—

As if   that sour and sweet sauce comes with a gold rush, the expanses
outside of these volcanic walls, the not here. Nestled in altitude,
a poster for Delgado Travel tantalizes: *España - Venezuela -
Jackson Heights*. A garish, wishful glow of.

Each time the Q or B or R train rattles by on the Manhattan Bridge, I close my windows to keep out the noise and dense, black dust.

The earth shattered in 1906, the sky roared ablaze. Our forefathers were paper sons, their birth certificates buried alive or burned in City Hall. They stepped forward, for each of our foremothers gave birth to 800 children. We were thus American. *We* attended clan hall meetings filled with strangers in everything but name, strangers in name only, who don't talk about—

I want to get to know my neighbors in Chinatown, especially the ones who grew up here. I want to know what this neighborhood was like before I arrived, before the bubble tea shops, before the art galleries. I want to, while ignoring those who ask where we are *really* from, to walk beside my neighbors down these streets, to be neighborly.

In the 1950s, Mao Zedong claimed that American imperialism was a paper tiger, outwardly fierce but *unable to withstand the wind and the rain*. Nikita Khrushchev replied that *the paper tiger has nuclear teeth*. In the 1960s, George Plimpton came back from Paris as a glowing paper lion, winking breezy hijinks, all the while an *agent of influence* at the CIA. In these naughts and teens, self-labeled paper tigers pay $1,450 each to learn: How To Romance Blond Women.

As if papers were these wispy gossamer nothings, tickets to role-playing games,

as if others could humor our pearl-white perils—when paperness demarcated our entire—

My father's documents misstate his birth place, his birth country, my mother's her birth date. Our realities become apocryphal.

Truly, there were no tiger mothers back then, nor tiger fathers, nor paper tigers. Unless you conflated our pronouns. My neighbors tell me stories of when they worked in the local sweatshops with their mothers, when they darted between and even swung from clothing racks. They hid from investigators coming by to make sure there were no child workers, in the folds of other people's disposable incomes, at the bottoms of buckets and barrels, out on the fire escape. Safety in cardboard, safety in numbers. When third grade meant *older*, that they could finally reach the sewing machine pedals on their tippy toes.

The *tigers*, by contrast, lived on the Upper East Side; they went to places like Wellesley and spoke with southern belle accents. They needed no certificates or family associations, for they had ringed fingers, mink stoles, and the ultimate Wade-Giles names, landing them on the cover of *Time*. May-Ling Soong boasted, *The only thing Oriental about me is my face.* Eleanor Roosevelt quipped, *She can talk beautifully about democracy. But she does not know how to live democracy.* Still, they were model Methodists, singing battle hymns in a 4/4 beat. Those who followed wound the same metronome, for emasculated science majors always sing in a minor key. The engineering method of a few, projected onto—

After Pearl Harbor, Warren Magnuson repealed exclusion, welcomed exactly 105 China-people a year. A travel ban that coagulated us, smooshed us together under a gavel.

Outside of English, we spoke completely different languages,

as if we toiled in a zero-sum game, sharing nothing but a hundred names. Cooking up massacred laundry. In 1964, my father set off for Brazil by cargo ship, taking three months to travel from L.A. to Panama to Curaçao to São Paulo. By the time he arrived, the military had seized the government in a coup.

To pay respect is not to come close to knowing. I long to pronounce the names of film directors in the same dialect, at least, to engage in a conversation in which we could nod acknowledgment to each other's respective circumstances. To know the signs to look for, to go beyond signs, migration patterns, bird calls, food habits and tastes in film. I can't sit still nor stand upright in the humidity. In lieu of asking where each of us came from, to have a sense of where each of us is coming from, even if we might. The arbitrary have precise consequences for those who remain labeled neither horse nor tiger. "We" post-'65ers yet another beast

as if the combination mutated us into donkeys. We cannot but attempt to fold these papers into the shapes of different animals, into the forms of different persons, our prepositional subjunctives doubled unto themselves.

I thought that the treasures and shells that mothers coo to their children were actually bundles of joy they kept close to them on their backs. I thought that the Chinese diaspora consisted of flowers and bridges,

As if there were an *ancient art of folding*, as *Confucius says*, of the
       possibility of redefinition. Numb me, number me, count me in,
as if we had no livers or eyeballs or bone marrow without laminated
       tree fibers. We take on the names of the deceased, give them
       new voices. When one grows up with another's name, the
       timbres striking loudest are whispers
              as simple as muffled giggles in the playground,
              as glorious,
              as anonymous,
              as exhaling

Tax Season

I am cultivating the fine art of pressed-for-time
dawdling. Twirling red tape around one's pinkie,
daydreaming of brackish water
and the moment before
myth makes a home in yours—

Did someone give you a cloak that infested the others?
Or have they lined your drawers for years?
Poised to flutter about,
dentists and banks and life savings—
a conversion of saving half-lives,
this financial purgatory so oddly American.
Teeth gleaming from these stiff uppers.
To wake up with the smell of enamel burning,
the grinding of whose toil insures these incisors, home salty home—

A social contract between state
& subject clenches a thousand-year-old alkalined egg,
translucent green artifice of what we thought
was pure, a tautological beginning.
To savor this urge and bury it—
an aporia of the no way in.

To ground myself, my otherwise dangling feet
rest on a hard, old-style rectangular suitcase,
with two clasps with large lock keyholes on the sides,
a worn, black leather handle in the middle. I store my old taxes
        inside.
I try to sit taller, upright.
Engineers of my beloved spreadsheet
creating new weapons of planned obsolescence
like ad men walking down Madison:

Incontrovertible morality so easily convertible.
Pull the top down, wash my mouth with some bubbling detergent,
cleanse my oxymoron. My people forever a task
of the imminent. At your service.

Stadium, Dam, Condo, Headquarters

To adopt or abort a sense of distance,
A disconnect from the rest of the world's tethers—
Chilling regulatory, private-*izations*.
Let us praise these infamous men. We were not there.

I saw him, he literally yelled his head off
Like a late-night manga character.
I figuratively bawled my eyes out
When he left. Such a cute, rosy-cheeked boy.
Collecting these heads and eyeballs, slicing
Work for a new Kippumjo House of Dolls Joy Division,
Smiling through gritted teeth in front of a future youth hostel.

Broadway is perfect for street-walking.
Bound in a nation-state of backwardness,
Or transgressed as a siren. Walking to the sidelines,
So that I don't need a permit. Lining my CV with red-colored tape.
Paper cuts killed our fleeing sons.

Deluge the leveed disasters,
Deconstruct them in futures market trends, in prose or fragment—
No amount of foot-dragging prevents me
From chipping away at my roof, a two-pronged
Hammer for our demise. Not even a shield.

What we were not—Whether, whither, weathered, beaten,
State subsidies for my private tests—meds—oil—fire—water—air,
Or a damned dam bestowed on me, gift-wrapped in vouchers.
Destruction you made my popular referendum.

Means-tested Manifesto

A surface sin, a tattooed connective tissue of thought
Or light, a skin effect of undulating conversations,
Current news head lice. Wavelengths saturate spines.

I skin dive for that which darkens by the sun.
I wear no suit, only a mask. It's figurative, I am afraid,
As skin-deep, as personal and sacred, as my skin.

A public sphere, a globule of difference.
No declared cells or flags in the shape of a sickle,
Nor a bigger slice of the pie nor a bigger pie.

No week or a month or March. No march
Or demonstration or PAC. No Pac-Man
Or grand theft. No automatic lists, less repeating.

Redundancy, thinking in a tank, statistically regressing
Analyses, shifting arms. Calling to them, to teach his own.
I'm holding a stake. I'll believe it when I dig it.

The color of my sickness, its colorblindness a guise, or
A disguise, *Hey hey hey, you can't catch me. I'm syntax-free.*
Skin taut by surgery. Taunted, who has a stake in my skin.

The Following are Proposed Facticities

Between you and me, larceny is da bomb.
Advocacy cannot be fair and balanced, only weighed.
The plasticity of his policies can be measured by pork barrels.
Social forces won't keep me from my newly laced bootstraps.

All capitalists are bloodsuckers, supplying demand for first cities.
Her heresy is committed with the sound of one hand flinching.
Your veracious mendacities flop like giant manatees. Oh the
    humanity.
My hypocrisy can be cured via daily injections of hypercrisy.

I wear cheap peasantries, sweatshop-embroidered blouses.
Your pumped-up fallacy has achieved a new, shiny allure.
My leprosy is a figurative force, attached to the nerves.
Modesty prevents her from linebreaking on the streets.

Facilities with identity formation render me the same.
Between legitimacy and co-optation, a fine crash pad.
Participatory governance is an endless teleconference.
Whimsy me citizen, human, or just barely so.

Postcarded in Cuba
Bahia de Matanzas, 2006

We came to visit the hospitals, to learn
How the locals live like the poor, die like the rich.
Dignify this vertiginous life-expectancy.
We see no US embassy, of course.
Only, an official special Interest on the esplanade,
Sleeping next to the monument to Elián.
Sometimes, a grave Concern. Almost disarming,
Heavily safeguarded by cruising men.
Black star flags stand in the way of Googled freedom.
A bloodletting for the bruised hearts of bombs.

Incandescent invincibles. *Mots justes*. In the absence of.
(Thinking back to all those rallying crowds at Union Square.
Not there, even. In the midst of shoe ads, dancing silhouettes.
Or big, multi-storied underwear people. Whole
American Virgin mega forever & noble mania warehouse.)
Mulled over, I carry a suitcase amygdala.

These balling, dancing folks tell me:
Home ownership rates mean nothing
Without entertaining plasma.
Universal health coverage won't fertilize
My music download collection.
Basketball is futile without Air Irans,

Or, as the English call them, trainers—
But my personal ones are closeted
In some epistemology of the covet.
Those skinny ass jeans are to die for.
Blunt transformations of my disconnect
A sort of pointy-toed slippered sadness.

In Beijing my friends joke that *schadenfreude*
Is actually a Chinese word. Or Esperanto.
Gleefully. WTO pacemakes annual growth.

I beg of you: Post-Soviet my brassiere, plea.
Honor this arrhythmia of my economic valves.

At the clinic, rectal ozone machines
Inflate my *special period*
A giant raft-hungry placebo.
The supposed end of neoliberalism,
A *perestroika* of homeopathy.
Ooh, & the beach is to die for.
Especially on these hot days, an ice cold war.

Block party! Bloc party.
The difference between *fiesta* and *partido* lies in.
You see, those committed to defending the Revolution
Feed me ruby soda and sweets.
(Awkwardly, the kids aren't allowed to partake in this.
Gracelessly, we embargo a cure to meningitis.
Who would have known, that this poor, poor...)
Grab my hands, twirl me ballooned wishes of love & love.
Greetings from the gorgeous view at waves lapping on
Matanzas is for lovers! Wish you were fear!

Cigars aren't allowed back,
Only "educational" souvenirs,
So I got you a dream-shaped procedure.

It's structurally adjusting my hyper-glycemic red.
On the way from. On the way from.
I cover my brains on the way to.
Oh *sub rosa* palimpsest. Your senses cry over my wet foot,
But my dry foot sinks deeper.

Coda

This, too, we mourn by forgetting.
Dubbed a crisis of *je ne sais quoi*, just as the phenomenon itself
    dissipates.

To simultaneously disappear and render difference,
A bitter, pickling kaffir lime *better*. To swallow myself whole.

(But I'd learned that naming
Made it true. Like an incantation, an acetylene force. Quick
    burning of

What I mean,
What I pine for, is a mean:
No absolutes, but a sense of proportion, my multitudes
    parliamentary.)

DISTANCES

A Book of
Questions

13

La Sebastiana, Valparaíso, Chile, 2006

Ravishing crocodiles also live in the Everglades, for they are
irresistible to Burmese pythons, which try to devour them whole.
Once the crocodile moves halfway down the python's digestive
track, they explode together. Some say they tear, or tear apart.

The oranges treat the sunlight as fantastical art, the tree as a
conflagration of excess humanity.

Acid mouths dribble sweet nothings shaped like Kissinger, and,
according to Bolaño, pigeon droppings.

(If I may.) Operation Condor officially began in 1975. Yet, this
home has sat empty since 1973. In other words, they proclaimed
that you passed naturally, of prostate cancer. In other words,
they killed you, on September 23rd, with a mysterious injection
to the stomach. We cast long shadows; they precede us with the
thorns of 60,000 police statutes.

To shed (less than skin, more than crocodile fears). I unravel
posthumous linings, flower-patterned pink silk, from my
threadbare jacket.

18

The grapes heard the party line through the grapevine, of course, shilling for raisins.

The challenge lies not in picking, but in planting right in the first place, in believing in process rather than in aptitude. We would all like to weave infinite filaments with the Three Fates, rocking back and forth on a veranda by the sea, but that is hardly pragmatic. They refused our offer of a filtration system. Who would pay the maintenance fees? We had not anticipated these questions. I stare at the whirring fan, try to remember the sensation called cold. You can give each citizen a fish or a Horatio Alger myth, but it is better to teach us to each crave Sizzler's Friday Night Special.

When we have renovated hell's dull rules—to run ablaze with shine, amidst our throngs of followers. No need for a reconstruction.

As Nixon's tapes reveal, the operative mode was not sadness, but anger. Atop a brazier, his buttocks would have merely flared pink with chagrin. But onward.

A conundrum of choice in being contemporary with a moment, but to ultimately escape its ill effects. No use to roasting Nixon over a small fire, marinated with napalm.

Let him rise back from Hades, move to Newark,
eat pão de queijo with newly arrived Brazilian families,
a fish every Friday for penance.
Allow each fish to come from the Passaic,
downstream from the Agent Orange factories he commanded.
May he go for the medium rare.

22

His ardor turned into an antelope-shaped ice sculpture, its taste and shape memorialized at film festivals all over Spain. Hers fossilized into ambivalent scorn, trapped under a notebook in Arkansas.

Whenever you wish to, you may conjure me. If I were little beside these digital images, serving as half-erased traces of whatever latest—or oldest—interpretation you attempt to inscribe in pixilated ink.

Global landscapes are not altered alone, or via central planning. Think of the big bowl in Brasília, the Cross-Bronx Expressway, the route between kitchen and bathroom where you live. I see the steps we have taken; our gloves sit listlessly at the bottoms of our drawers, bins, knapsacks. My hands are frostbitten, his bear the burns from last summer. Still, this is migration, this is the making of homes.

These days, Beijing counts the number of "blue sky days" each year on a single hand. Acrid yellow sandstorms from Ulaanbaatar lash against Tokyo, against Juneau, against San Francisco. The waters no longer sing.

51

In such cities, we stand outside ourselves, and the streets are awash in pheromones, the fetid smell of the *homo sacer*, violently murdered but not sacrificed. Mere footsteps from those accursed. Hallowed hearts beating, brains functioning, alive. The odor emanates from the architecture, from the primordial, anything but. We do not lose our senses, only our masks.

Each small sea of plasticities, of aspirations, of immobilities rises to a new level each year. On the arctic waterfront lie chemical villages, the only places in the world where baby girls outnumber baby boys.

She was called "a civilized wind," without the superstitions of wind and water.

For it is better to claim grievances against an indifferent state than to have no place. We are limitless, yes, and thus, so easily swept, as if nibbling on plankton at the bottom of this ocean.

64

Our faded clothes flutter like flags from fast fashion, from
two-week hyper-ventilations between design, pattern-making,
manufacturing, shipment, marketing, display, and purchase,
satiation, cheapness. Worn from travel, from want, from
symbolism and a dearth of color and acquiescence.

I cannot fathom whether the refugees we see on the news
broadcasts, the ones who chat amiably with reporters on
trains, who have learned bits of Korean from K-pop songs or
telenovelas, who all seem to speak fluent English, who dream
of Germany, are sometimes evil, and always good, and utterly
different from who they were yesterday.

We are not the sort to pray. This is what we pray against: Five
sodas and four telephone calls on the Spanish border. In this,
the mask of kindness—we cry for them, for they are surprisingly
blond, for they remain across the Atlantic, for they are not the
ones in Maine, in Colorado, in Minnesota.

Those who cite Baudelaire are but skin-toned. The flowers of
good, on the other hand, trick us with their ultraviolet rays,
their translucence, as if adhered onto a drape of innocence,
accessorized deservingness.

In Břeclav, in the Czech Republic, women in baseball caps and
police uniforms with twinkling white stars number the women
and children with indelible markers. We cannot help but gasp
at the sight, a contemporary rendition of the Monrovian town
just seventy years ago, less than a lifetime ago, but the head
coverings flag the trespasses novel, unadorned.

TERRITORIES

The 403 is Not Verboten
After the HTTP 403 Forbidden error page

What we wish for is hangout chat messaged deliberation, this conjoining with the other. For it seems that every December, I send out postcards wishing friends "serendipity and delight." In return, the postal service sends blank stares—because, I conjecture, these sentiments sound shallow, clichéd. In Aleppo, Damascus, Arakan, Juarez, Spotify, Forgetify, CryptoParty this: An echo chamber of my "favorite" friends' "thoughts," *all links and no thresholds*. Clickbait my slacktivist. My fingers do the balking, and my synapses remain. (We wander towards another. The glass is always cleaner there.)

Being alone together is different from walking in rush hour at Penn Station, from standing without tongues locked at a New Year's party. It is to have one's intestines illuminated primarily, not solely, by the wet streaks of one's fears. *The body is an evolutionary architecture that operates and becomes aware in the world. To alter its architecture is to adjust its awareness.* A tattoo in the color of belonging, a binary code for what will never.

Like Pessoa, we have usernames, dozens of avatars. Bots remind us to change passwords once a month, to speak new acronymic languages as mnemonic devices for no one but for "people," for *Citizens United*. I download an app that turns my screens from blue to orange at night, as if my eyes dart back and forth any less during golden hour. We implant subcutaneous chips into our beloved black Labradors, so that they are always found. Perhaps our beloved 2 year-old toddlers, too, those wandering terribles. These snarkphones tethered to our fingertips. This system positions me globally. It says—buy this dress instead of that one; it has been placed here for you. You can turn off a mobile device, but not a stratagem.

Tabaski on the African Fairhaven
Ile de Gorée, 2013

1. Signoras

A friend advised me to come here partly because
it's quiet here, unlike on the mainland.
It seems quiet here. It *seems*
quiet here, the quiet punctuated by whirs of occasionally larger
    waves lapping in,
shrieks of happiness as children play on the beach,
dare one another to go a bit farther out.

Some called it *Ber*. The Dutch, *Good Reed*.
The Portuguese, *Ilha da Palma*.
(Today, I saw few outside of the capitalist ersatz.
The GSM towers are not quite disguised as tall, gray palm trees.)

The French, *good harbor*, or so says the BBC.
The island is haunted with pop songs, with trinkets, with mythologies.
In *McBride's*, October 1876, an article on "the African Fairhaven"—
David Livingstone says a "slave-stick" is known as a gorée,
a "forked log" to push slaves from the interior,
out to this edge.

Such a log works with harnesses, fury.
McBride's reprints a British sailors' ditty:
    I've a spanking wife at Portsmouth gates,
        A pigmy at Gorée,
    An orange-tawny up the Straits,
        A black at St. Lucie:
    Thus whatsomedever course I bend,
        I leads a jovial life:

snaps, ขาย ("sell") ปลา ("fish"). 3000 miles to the north, a teenager sweet-talks to her hot, new, industrializing

In every mess I find a friend,
In every port a wife.

Next to a house that played a "minimal" role in passages,
displaying all of the trinkets of a beach boardwalk. The *signoras*,
the *senhoras* built this house. Fashionable madams
in bustled dresses, commanding male clerks in tall wigs.

Towards the back of the complex, a long corridor, a door shape
of sky at the end   a dreamscape

    I take one step, two,   stop.
    Keep myself from lurching forward.
There is no beach sand outside, no railing, no stoop.
The door perched on a cliffside, a platform for an Olympic dive,
    a double twist into—

Gde CELLULE DES
RECALCITRANTS

in the global quilt, lining superhighways with electric cables, dotting backroads with mini-malls

These rooms would barely fit queen-sized beds,
let alone—how many—minimal—bodies—people.

By the pink salt lake,
amidst the gum arabic, the ivory, the peanut oil, the gold-dust,
    the wives.
One *salle* is for *les filles*, but the one to the right is for the *young* girls.

This bare emptiness—two meters by two meters
of concrete, if that—too small to fathom.
And across a small courtyard, a room for *the recalcitrants*.

What,   but
sanity,   but
cognition,   but
functional synapses and capillaries,   but
anything,   but
could deign them recalcitrant, assorted
with the chill of labeled ages and attitudes,
set to the tune of a salty song.

Tourists visit each dilapidated mansion.
Marshmallow peep canary yellows, French doors, windowless boxes
      onto sobbing blues
each emblazoned with the graffitied refrain, *ca$h money*.
The smell of *plenty, infinity.* Beyond.

Local girls and boys dive off piers, into games
of Marco Polo, into the color turquoise.

Even just days before Tabaski, the goats are safe here.
Clean. An accent to our idyll.

Notes on the Shape of Absence

We trace the dust lines left behind from the appliances, fumble for the brick foundations between the steel beams, peer at serrated stairlines where the wall paints stopped. Reincarnated. Tenement apartments become dance spaces without barres or mirrors, in the dank basement of a bank on Market Street, in anonymous green-carpeted rooms on Mott Street.

The first time I met WM,
she told me,

*There were three main theaters
that my family and I would go to:
the Music Palace on Bowery, the
Sun Sing on East Broadway, and
the third one by the Manhattan
Bridge whose name I've since
forgotten and which is now a
Buddhist temple...*

*All of them played martial arts
movies, ghost stories, and soft-
core porn (there was some kind
of two-for-one ticket thing to
do with the latter).*

I found a *Life Magazine* spread about Sun Sing. It started off as the Florence New Strand Theatre in 1921, hosting Yiddish-language vaudeville.

In 1940, a professional opera troupe from Hong Kong arrived. World War II broke out, so the troupe got stranded here. They took over the theater and performed every night. Death, resurrection, applause. I try to imagine what Claude Lévi-Strauss thought as he sat in the audience, draw a causal pathway between these events.

In 1942, the same year as that *Life Magazine* spread, the company changed the theater's name to New Canton, and made its last appearance.

for hearts and minds. Often an essentializing process, sometimes not. I hope to encounter, amidst the

New Canton became a cinema and was renamed Sun Sing Theatre again in 1950. In the late 1970s and early 1980s, more non-Chinese folks showed up, with Chinese-language subtitles on top and English-language subtitles on the bottom.

In 1993, Sun Sing closed. *Enter the Wu-Tang (36 Chambers)*, featuring English dub audio samples from *Shaolin and Wu Tang* (1983) and *The 36th Chamber of Shaolin* (1978), hit stores. In *The 36th Chamber*, Yude becomes San Te, learning kung fu in each of the Shaolin temple's 35 chambers. Later, after helping his hometown defeat a brutal Manchurian general, he establishes the eponymous chamber, where the sacred can become a popular art form of resistance.

Last I checked, Sun Sing had been demolished to make room for a shopping mall peddling cell phone accessories. (At night, the dim sum palace across the street hosts dance parties, replete with fog machine.)

Haunted Karaoke. Fascination Amour. Kickboxer's Tears.

In 1998, the top-grossing feature films in the US were *Saving Private Ryan, Armageddon*, and *There's Something About Mary*. Cheap DVD knock-offs made it easy for immigrants to gain access to Hong Kong movies in the comfort of their own homes. The Music Palace closed.

It's a lonely job, but it's a nice job. I like being the guy up in the booth.

In the past, no seats were available. You had to stand to watch. We probably had one thousand people at a time.

A Vitasoy is 75 cents.

When you are here alone, without your family, you either rest or go to work, working overtime. You just have to buy one ticket, and you can stay here all day.

The Pagoda became an HSBC bank branch, the Sun Sing became a mall. One of the Music Palace's new owners told *Sing Tao Daily* in 2005 that he found and put aside between 400 and 500 old film reels before the building was demolished. The 18-story Wyndham Garden hotel replacing the Music Palace also displaced 50 low- and moderate-income residents next door.

not the push but the pushback. For the right to be somewhere, to take up space, to be rezoned into

existence. The exact paths of my daily perambulations are not dictated by formal laws and structures.

Our routine was to buy a packet of watermelon seeds and eat the entire bag while watching the films, and the seed husks would crunch beneath our feet when we left. Mom spent most of the time chasing me throughout the theater because I wouldn't sit still. One movie that's stayed with me was of Sally Yeh being gang-raped and then exacting a total and utter martial-arts revenge on the gang. (I think she fails at the first attempt, gets assaulted again, and then rises up again and finally kills them all.)

but enforcement and access. I jaywalk. These routes we trample into reality despite the absence of

In real life, I am told, my mother was not a phoenix, for phoenixes do not exist.

It is not as if we spoke each Sunday evening, so that I could properly miss her then. Her absence is not conspicuous. There is no definition, I cannot define it, *i.e.*, I am at a loss for meaning. I constantly play a personal *Mad, Mad Libs*: I am living for ___(noun, verb)___ . I cannot think of loss without falling into platitudes, specificities, Bishop's elusive art. When rhythms provide a cooing, a rocking back and forth, tender pain a painful tenderness, traipsing across the board at 45-degree angles, telling it slant.

Officially, we pay tribute when it is clear and bright: the paulownia begins to bloom, voles transform into quails. Somehow, with eerie consistency, we stand under low cloud cover, winds chilling us to our bones, despite the mild temperatures. Rainbows begin to appear.

Each evening, I sink into my bed, contemplating what I did not accomplish today.

She told me to build a shrine to my jaw, that which I whittled away, ground to arthritis. Lying like a biological pile of carpenters' off-cut, the width of that marked line that always curls to the ground. This irrepressible feeling, a primordial pyrrhic catarrh. It flares along borderlands, only in between. (An Elean paradox, every moment I am nearly, I am merrily, I am alive.)

And so, our hands are long. But she called narratives Sisyphian. Each time I pause typing, my chair rolls backward on the sloped floor. In a moment of magic, I thought that she simply withheld authorial power.

the small dam by the lake, for make-out sessions. I think of the dirt paths next to the sidewalks, next

The facts do not change,

for   they are constantly rewritten.

The ghostly Gowanus roofline I admired, now a Whole Foods store,
complete with rooftop garden,
atop a Superfund site. What remains
seeps into the soil, and our veins.

Hydrogen, carbon, and oxygen spin flashbacks into gray entrails,
weaving lines of spice into the air. When the capricious gases
are irascible enough, the social ties break apart, and the atoms
breathe again to turn wet, to exhale carbon dioxide. In other
words, they burn. Charred sweet, the carbs sometimes turn to
cakey nostalgia, but more slowly. This is why shish kebabs from
Brazil linger on the mind's tongue.

Carbon atoms emit air.

(But   this only works when you dream that you are dreaming of
nostalgia, or fire.)

In Thailand, in a corner of each plot of land, the owners build spirit houses to appease the spirits who once dwelled there. Figurines overflow from the opulent ones.

The simplest, built by Burmese refugees on the edge of the forest, or those in more isolated environments, strike me hardest.

In ancient Rome, similar houses were built for *Lares Familiares*. Our dead mothers live there, but when we seek greener pastures, higher offices, they stay put.

B, easements by necessity, easements by prescription. Along these paths, not a possibility but a

If we could have miniatures on every block of the homes, say, that the Atlantic Yards Barclay's Center replaced, or those that Robert Moses demolished to make way for the Cross-Bronx Expressway, with overpasses too low for public buses to pass under, so that Jones Beach could remain white.

I read that this was once the home of—

I cannot differentiate the homage from the lament. As I resign, I surmise. More often than not, via whitewashing or semiotic deconstruction, the erasure.

Sometimes, these virtual landscapes feel realer than

Were we to name names alongside black rectangles to symbolize
our mourning

Were we to   combat the mundane ferocity that prefigures
    the rough ride
        (He testified to his 22-month-old self)
    he testifies to his   (knowing)
        The windows, paint was peeling off the windows.

    I mull and articulate too slowly. By then,
everyone else has covered the essential angles.
    I summon my voice to join the outrage,

Tangential weapon, ersatz activism with
        the bend of an index finger. I   "like"   it
        because I am exhausted,   because I long for
          polyphonic   song

This is not yet sacrifice
        yet resistance
        abolition
        a refrain
        from

            Each of us slumps forward
                tracing parallels.

sit. Searching for these interstitial spaces, to be public without sanction, without broken windows, the

Mothers at altitude
Mothers in solitude
Mothers as platitude
Mothers in spring

Mothers ashamed and Ablaze and clear
At the end
As they are
As they almost all are, and then
Mothers don't come around
Again in spring

Anne Carson

But   what is clear is invisible.
        What is weightiest remains intangible.

        The difference is not that I do not know,
but   that I never will.   I track most carefully what I cannot see.
        Opening one's eyes wide is not seeing,
but   believing.   No witnessing to bear and hold up on
                        my fingertips to the window, the low blue light
                        and long shadows of early April.

As if   I could listen to the silence (for silence

assumes the cadence of one's last gasping breaths,

synesthetic roar),

inadequate morphine, we succumb to negative space, stoop
   lower with each breath.

When I was younger, I dreamt of shine.
In my mind's eye, I glittered,
an optical illusion nearing the truth, more truthfully an alluring
   asymptote.

I refracted, proffered all

these shards of glass.

powerstrips during Sandy. In Bangkok, a group of five young people—not quite an official assembly—

Aubade: At the Bus Shelter

We are neither here, nor there.
We are horse horse tiger tiger.
We are snake snake fish fish.
We are more or less.
We are like this, like that.
We are so-so.

We are not pineapple,
        nor the apples of anyone.
Our eyes are not windows, and
our souls are not bread.
Our hands wave royally.

This is no sleight of hand.
Because I am left-handed, gauche but not sinister,
the still-damp ink of each word I write smears
as my hand skims the paper
to write the next word.
More than fingerprints, the printer's mark of the side of
my hand a signature—
        more than joy or anguish, except, perhaps, hunger,
    or ennui, or saudade—that
we are living,
as if   we are not quite alive.

We are marginalia.
We lie between the lines, the fine print of
our social contracts.

Our votes are not cast,
but   one day,
our children will be special electorates.
We hear that they will go to a special college.

We are soaring American.
We are standing united.
We are going transcontinental. Between points A and B,
we pray to the oracle of delta.

when, because the ground beneath our feet no longer holds, we anticipate what is simultaneously

Ghost Streets

In São Paulo, we visited Supermercado Eldorado each Sunday—
turning in our Coca-Cola bottles, checking out the latest milk
    prices,
their strings of zeroes.

This sheaf of bills now
represents these numbers, which represent these values
not there—apparent—yesterday.
My reward is sitting on a bar stool, experiencing heartburn for the
    first time:
The excitement of feijoada and moqueca, *yes* to farofa on top.
In my mind, I replaced *farofa* with *alfafa* for twenty-one years.

On the news, each evening at eight—
the official currency exchange,
& the real, "black market" one. Jotting down both numbers to
    report to my parents.
Whereby each official statement punches us in the gut not as a lie,
nor a remaking of reality,
but   the constant disconnects between
    the official   the "real"   normalized.
We did not need different news sources to make this happen.

My brother and I wore matching brown Mickey Mouse sweatsuits
to the consulate in Rio. We were sponsored by my real aunt, in
good faith. In the middle of the night, on the overnight bus back
home, I swallowed a large, green hard candy before I was ready to.
At the airport, I revealed the secret stash of children's chewable

multivitamins to the security guard, rolled up inside our clothes;
she took the half that was hers, plus a hair-dryer. Then, I learned
to introduce myself and force a bucktoothed smile, to shop
clerks, with only the official truths, documented with seals.

what is not yet evident, wearing galoshes on the terrain of a genre of science nonfiction. Given what

In Manhattan, beneath counterfeit handbags and noodle restaurants, a canal flowed.

To survive a near-death experience, I attempted to operate not according to feelings/ facts, but thoughts/ acts. It is not *as if* I could be off the grid, hermetically sealed, deactivating the non-erasures. Abstention here as realistic as abstinence.

I have   lived
(__ years, x 365.25 days, x 24 hours, and)
I am now here.
I have   earned   my certificate hours of existence/
     my right to a shadow,
to   permit it to follow me around,
to   speak with authority w/o
                disclosing autobiographical secretions,
                placing my drool on public display.

In Los Angeles, between Sunset and Fountain, we trace a hypotenuse. Once, people I have never met rode rails there, traipsed around   curvilinear.

To   navigate no parallels, nor perpendiculars, but easements. Unfolding a map of common laws: A record of damage, etched into the shapes of our buildings. That which could not be coded into our geographical information systems, codified in white with a knife and a fork, flattened into sociological tropes. In my dreams, words travel here,

but   they do not arrive. I pray that my movements and thoughts remain   opaque to all
but   you. My existence recognized through affect rather than visibility, hyper-. Between seeing and a cunning of recognition, you shift my reflex from *bristle*,

to.   From   moment
to   moment
to   moment
to.

four steps ahead. A few weeks before we moved to the US, my mother taught me the alphabet in

oun-Of-Tunis

Sunset Grill

Ralp

Sunset

G

Sunset 5

Meltd

and C

Sam A

Music S

y Guitars

a Vista

The

Momen

N. Martel Av

Desire Lines

To imagine what I would,

as if   I could

move beyond paranoid deconstruction
of the city in which I live, of its decapitation of hills. Leveling.

To build holloways,
to cut fences with precision pliers, to bushwhack, to scramble
    the rocks,
to find a new way to the pond's edge.

After snowfall, the existing paths are invisible,
the street noise white. I listen to my now "innocent" heart murmur,
transcribe each pump—a washy cymbal sounding off
                    an excess beat
of oxygenated blood whooshing back—
with a slow step, snow crunching underfoot.

I look at my footprints, I photograph them with my phone.
I try to connect the dots of my treads,
speculate the shape of my disobedience.
The shortest days cast the longest shadows,
my double trailing far behind me in the early afternoon.

English; I learned the Germanic letters *k*, *x*, and *y*. But they dismiss our testimonies, because we/our

JFK Airport

I am delayed   I am canceled
I have a license   I have a passport
the picture is mine   I come
in good faith   She is my *bona fide*
blood filial   my only   I have no other
names   here is the stamp   I have
this hologram   I have
a destination   I speak some Spanish because
the signature is mine   I have
a sense of direction   I have
a purpose   I was born there because
I have   a spleen
to vent   I'm willing myself
to remember the physical sensation called home*coming*,
called home*sickness*   I am an assemblage of maybes
I must run to the gate   please let me through
I will become   I have an appointment to keep

Here, on the eastern tip
of the Brooklyn-Queens border, even after
each new court injunction against 45's travel ban,
the guards operate
as if   we lurk

                    in   but not of
America. Supermodernity is under constant renovation.
My "inalienable" right to refuse police access to my phone
has dissipated into the dry airport air.
This is a port of entry to—

the possibilities of free trade zones, superior political zones.
I brace myself for extra questioning each time I re-enter the US.
(Just now, I almost write "return home" instead of "re-enter the
US," but a slight ache below my diaphragm stops me.) Fear

shoots a prickly pain down my legs.
One day, it will knock me to the floor, pleading
ignorance, or exhaustion, or—

When I grow up. My fingerprints, keys to the cloud, the wires resting in the darkness of ocean floors,

EXIT

EXIT

EXIT

EXIT

EXIT

I first arrived on a Pan Am flight.
I thought of it as liberatory,
a fugitive glimpse of a utopian city-world, where
I could discard rules and scripts, my scraping by.

As if   I could get un-situated
this airport a bubble hovering
in a void between celestial bodies
                    in   but not of
the country I stand in. Now,
I pass through the metal detector,
the gender verification machine with a blast of air.
I do not request the special pat-down alternative.
I walk to the left on the moving sidewalks.
I allow the compressed air to stick to the back of my throat,
relishing that for once, I am not supposed to do anything
but   arrive early, occupy space-time—

tucked in the open desert. Hiding in and of plain sight, a right to have rights, even here, away from

I think of other airports, note what is missing here:
the choice between sitting and squatting,
hundreds of paintings of Prince by local high school students
    lining the corridors,
signs pointing to the direction in which Mecca lies.
A square, jewel box of a room in the middle of a terminal, all
    glass walls,
filled with cigarette smoke. Three smokers inside, careful to
    avoid each other's eyes,
not knowing where to look
without the comfort of opaque walls.

Paper Streets

Let me clip your bangs and clip them to this clipboard.
Let me dust the shelves, clean them thoroughly,
let me dust the pan with powdered sugar, coat it evenly with
"sweet"—"facially neutral"—"colorblind."

The state has sanctioned our industry to do this,
we fear it will sanction us for following through.
To be nonplussed is the new nonplussed.
This documentation of streets and -scapes
a product of not enough deep sleep, too much REM sleep,
    early morning
lucid dreaming about turning the corners of endless corridors,
fingers tracing the divets of pale green, simulated concrete
    bricks along the walls.
To be disconcerted is the new concerted.
To be both is to be permanently neither,
but,   she said, *documentation is intervention.*

Our new governances demarcate the grids
& topographies of our un-navigable days.
Legal clarity obfuscates only
what is possible, as if paper and air could possibly meet
at the markets, shake invisible hands in mediation.
I unsee stores on the streets, recognize only what I can afford.
This is called "zoning out." To come to my senses, I stare
out my bedroom window, at a point in the middle distance—
a comforting gray water tower.

   donors, others resident aliens. Pink card for Shan refugees, blue card for hilltribe Indigenous peoples,

But   reflections of our daily commutes   conscribed   into easements,
       untrammeled   ungraveled,   our politics of   future.

                        The tower is obscured on one side
by the oxidized green copper turrets of a church steeple,
wrapped in scaffolding, netting. On the other side,
rectangular slabs with jagged tops like Lego blocks, growing taller
    every few days.
This property has been subsumed by its neighbors; it is zoned
    for—

Trap Streets

A map is not the territory,
but it becomes so over time.
Just north of Roscoe, New York, the cartographers
Otto G. Lindberg and an assistant, Ernest Alpers,
named the town of Agloe after an anagram of their initials.
Rand McNally subsequently included their fantasy town
in *its* road maps, too—
Its company surveyors clearly copying and pasting,
too motionless to plot the area themselves.

But the non-existence of the town of Agloe, the courts deemed, is
a non-copyrightable fact.
    Finders keepers, they begged.
    And we mixed our labor with the soil!
It was too late. The local Exxon
only too keen on naming itself after this fantastical place,
at the intersection of Highway 206 & Morton Hill Road.

We lay down these lines
in green as camouflage, to catch others in the act of mimicry.
These two essences of blending, in labor, in yearning,
in naming our new little bodega after what we read in books,
coloring just outside the lines.

borders. Instead, they became luminescent, seeping into dreams whenever. Masters of bridled

We meant it only
as a quirk, a splash of color, a tribute to an old flame,
our fingerprints, our football rivalries, our silent aspirations.
But   our most personal rituals and customs become
codified on customs forms,
our duty-bound friendships and ecologies of care duty-free
only in liquor shops at the border.
> *(To become legible,* he whispered,
> *is to be tamed into a taxable animal.)*

A state of emergency is no state of exception. This law envelops
us in its warm, soft statutes. Looking out onto the horizon for
the there, there.
But   New Caledonia appears only on Google Earth, despite
Captain James Cook's claims.
Its longitude and latitude warn us of volcanoes, of Tonga, of
what we claim to know.

Notes

Route 1095 Italicized lines are excerpts from the Burmese Refugee Project / Kwah Dao children's essays, especially from 2004.

Seeing Like a State This poem is inspired in part by James C. Scott's *Seeing Like a State*. Parts of this poem are inspired by oral histories I conducted with May Wong Lee, Thomas Yu, and Susan Yee via the Asian American Writers' Workshop Open City initiative. Quotations by public figures were culled from popular press pieces archived online.

Means-tested Manifesto Part of the italicized line is from "The Ineffable Me" by Sonic Youth.

Postcarded in Cuba The "American Interests Section" in Havana became an embassy again in 2015. When I visited in 2006, there were lines of visa applicants outside, and lots of patrolling soldiers. Across the street, the Cuban government erected billboards criticizing the American government & its policies, including specific clauses of No Child Left Behind. The Bush administration put up its own electronic billboard ticker, featuring seemingly randomly assorted quotations on "freedom"— as if they had Googled "freedom" and posted whatever came up. In response, the Cuban government erected black flags that obscured the electronic billboard. Elsewhere in the city, I was particularly struck by the pronounced absence of marketing materials, advertisements. There were only billboards with statements like, *Las ideas justas son invicibles*. (Just ideas are invincible.)

Distances I first wrote the poems in this section as reflections upon Pablo Neruda's *The Book of Questions*.

The 403 is Not Verboten The first italicized line is by John Beckmann, from "Merge invisible layers," found *Virtual Dimension* edited by John Beckmann, published by Princeton Architectural Press, 1998. The second italicized line is by Stelarc, from *Zombies & Cyborgs: The Cadaver, the Comatose & the Chimera*, written in 2004, available at http://web.stelarc.org/texts.html.

Tabaski on the African Fairhaven The ditty and some of the details were published in the article "An African Fairhaven," in *McBride's* magazine, Volume 18, October 1876, pp. 414-425.

Notes on the Shape of Absence Some of the italicized stanzas are excerpts from an oral history with Wah-Ming Chang, conducted with the Asian American Writers' Workshop Open City initiative. Some of the italicized lines are quotes by the staff of the Music Palace (lines transcribed from Eric Lin's short documentary, *Music Palace*)—Ho Ying Pang (manager), Jian Bang Wang (assistant manager), Dave Butterman (projectionist).

In the line "the paulownia begins to bloom…," I refer to the three pentads of Qing Ming ("clear and bright"), the 5th solar term of the East Asian lunisolar calendar. This is the traditional time of the year when families visit the tombs of the deceased. It usually falls on the first week of April.

The line "The windows, paint was peeling off the windows" comes from Freddie Gray, killed by hypervisible, fast violence in a "rough ride." I am thinking also of Rob Nixon's notion of slow violence, from *Slow Violence and the Environmentalism of the Poor,* and how Gray himself worked to address this slow violence, and gradual and often invisible killings, by testifying in his 2008 lawsuit against his absentee landlord. Scientists state that blood lead levels of 5 micrograms per deciliter cripple cognitive development, decrease IQ, impair memory. In June 1991, when Gray was 22 months old, his blood carried 37 micrograms. I first read these details in "Freddie Gray's Life a Study on the Effects of Lead Paint on Poor Blacks" by Terrence McCoy, published in the *Washington Post,* April 29, 2015.

Aubade: At the Bus Shelter Some phrases for something being so-so, tolerable: comme ci comme ça (like this like that), más o menos (more or less), 馬馬虎虎 (horse horse tiger tiger), งูๆปลาๆ (snake snake fish fish), ไม่เป็ (it's not pineapple).

Ghost Streets This poem is inspired in part by Edouard Glissant's "right to opactiy for everyone," from *Poetics of Relation.*

The phrase "cunning of recognition" is inspired by Elizabeth Povinelli's book with this phrase as its title.

Desire Lines This poem is inspired in part by Eve Kosofsky Sedgwick's *Touching Feeling,* and her analyses of paranoid and reparative critique.

JFK Airport The line "in but not of" is from and in part inspired by *The Undercommons: Fugitive Planning and Black Study* by Stefano Harney and Fred Moten, as well as critical examinations of varying shadow states.

The line "a fugitive glimpse of a utopian city-world" is by PD Smith in his discussion of *Non-Places: Introduction to an Anthropology of Supermodernity* by Marc Augé, published in *The Guardian,* March 28, 2009.

Acknowledgments

Grateful acknowledgement is made to the editors of these publications where versions of some of these poems first appeared: *580 Split, 88: A Journal of Contemporary American Poetry*, Academy of American Poets *Poem-a-Day, Action, Yes, Aufgabe, Almost Five Quarterly, Boston Review, Brooklyn Rail, Drunken Boat, The Margins, Open City, Sand, Sous Rature, Truck, XCP: Cross-Cultural Poetics, Zócalo Public Square*, and *Devouring the Green: Fear of a Human Planet: An Anthology of New Writing* (Jaded Ibis Press, 2015). Many thanks to Belladonna* for publishing some of these poems in the chapbook *Beyond Relief*, and to Éireann Lorsung of MIEL Books for publishing part of this book in the chapbook *Plurality Decree*.

All images are by me and/or Kiran Puri, except for the following, reprinted with profuse thanks: The essay reprinted in "Route 1095" is by one of the children I worked with in the Burmese Refugee Project/ Kwah Dao. In "Notes on the Shape of Absence," the photo of the architectural palimpsest is by Eva the Weaver; images of the Music Palace cinema are stills from the documentary *Music Palace*, directed by Eric Lin. In "Ghost Streets," a screenshot of Marshfield Way in Los Angeles, on Google Maps.

Thank you to the Millay Colony for the Arts, Saltonstall Colony for the Arts, Ucross Foundation, Asian American Writers' Workshop, Center for Book Arts, and the Community of Literary Magazines and Presses Face Out program for fellowships and support.

My deepest thanks to Caroline Crumpacker, Ana Paula Simões, Rachel Levitsky, Krystal Languell, and the Belladonna* Collaborative, and also to Kiran Puri and HR Hegnauer. To Paul Beatty, Cindi Katz, Alissa Quart, Dorothy Wang, for your generous support. My immense gratitude to all those I have worked with over the years, some of whom became close friends and adopted family, who shared these literal and figurative and hoped-for migrations and borderlands and landias with me.... It is an honor to share stories with you, to recognize and map livelihoods, the ways in which lived experience might rub against what is sanctified. Thank you to my friends on the border, to Roj, Kaan, NaNa, NeNe, Nuan, Artit, Jab, Taworn, Khong, Kamloo, Pao, Sangkor, Pai, Swaymud, Amporn, and your families. To my old neighbors and friends in Chinatown and the Lower East Side, to all of you who work every day for a right to the city, a right to have rights, you have taught me more than you know. To attempt to engage with humility and radical vulnerabilities, to create placeholders for us to imagine otherwise. Thank you to Tim Carrier, Wah-Ming Chang, Paolo Javier, Ben Lerner, and Althea Wasow, for your incisive readings and insights that contributed to this book. To those, named and unnamed, who have nourished me with your friendship over the years. Thank you, always, to my brother Alex Su, my father Caleb Su, Ellen Blinder, Russell Blinder, Elise Blinder, Katie Bradley, Collin Blinder, Lan Ho, Helen Wu, Brian Wu, Andy Schlesinger, Jonathan VanDyke, Ben Ho, Romina Wahab, Esther Wu, and Wesley Wu for your family embrace. To my mom, Christina Su, who taught *light* by conviction. To Justin Blinder, a material state of belonging.

About the Author

Celina Su was born in São Paulo, Brazil, and lives in Brooklyn. Her writing includes two poetry chapbooks *Plurality Decree* (MIEL Books, 2015) and *Beyond Relief* (with Ariana Reines, Belladonna*, 2013), three books on the politics of social policy and civil society, and pieces in journals such as *n+1*, *Harper's*, and *Boston Review*. Su is the Marilyn J. Gittell Chair in Urban Studies and an Associate Professor of Political Science at the City University of New York. She has received several distinguished fellowships, including a Berlin Prize and a Whiting Award for Excellence in Teaching. This is her first book of poetry.